D0394069

TIMELINES

1970s

by
Jane Duden

CRESTWOOD HOUSE

New York

Library of Congress Cataloging In Publication Data
Duden, Jane.
   1970s / by Jane Duden.
   p. cm. — (Timelines)
   Includes index.
   Summary: History, trivia, and fun through photographs and articles present life
in the United States between 1970 and 1979.
   ISBN 0-89686-478-2
   1. United States—History—1969- —Miscellanea—Juvenile literature. 2. History,
Modern—1945- —Miscellanea—Juvenile literature. [1. United States—History—
1969- —Miscellanea.] I. Title. II. Series: Timelines (New York, N.Y.)
E855.D83   1989   973.92—dc20   89-34630
                                                CIP
                                                AC

Photo credits
Cover: Journalism Services: Tall ships sail up New York Harbor for the Bicentennial
   Celebration
FPG International: 4, 14 (right), 34
Wide World Photos: 6, 8, 9, 11, 12, 13, 14 (left), 15, 17, 19, 20, 21, 23, 24, 25, 26, 27, 28, 31, 32,
   36 (right), 37, 38, 39, 40, 43, 45, 46
The Bettmann Archive: 36 (left)
DRK Photo: (Annie Griffiths) 31

Macmillan Publishing Company
866 Third Avenue
New York, NY 10022
Collier Macmillan Canada, Inc.

CRESTWOOD HOUSE

Produced by Carnival Enterprises

Printed in the United States of America

First Edition

10 9 8 7 6 5 4 3 2 1

CONTENTS

INTRODUCTION

The 1970s were a decade of space exploration and new rights for women and blacks. They were also a time when science had a greater effect than ever before on people's lives. After the turmoil of the sixties, the "me generation" searched for personal fulfillment and self-discovery. But people also spoke up about protecting the environment and conservation. Health and fitness fads like running and yoga took off and became big business. Blue jeans became the national uniform, topped off by T-shirts with slogans. Political scandal brought the first resignation of an American president and distrust of government. The public turned to new leadership — the Democrat Jimmy Carter — for a change. The unpopular Vietnam War finally came to an end. Inflation drove the cost of living higher and higher. The decade also gave birth to superstars in rock music, movies, and sports. The seventies saw great change in everything from politics to personal values.

Demonstrations against the Vietnam War continued into the seventies.

A PRE-GAME TOUCHDOWN

It was Super Bowl Sunday, January 11, 1970. The Minnesota Vikings were pitted against the Kansas City Chiefs in New Orleans. Before the game, two hot air balloons took off from the field. A Vikings fan piloted one of the balloons. A Chiefs fan piloted the other. The balloons were supposed to float out of the stadium. Unfortunately, the balloon flown by the Vikings fan became caught in the stands. Fans tore at the balloon, making forty-foot holes in it. The Vikings were hit once again when the Chiefs trounced the Vikings, 23-7.

SHOOTINGS SHOCK NATION

Four students demonstrating at Kent State University in Ohio were shot dead on May 4 by troops of the United States National Guard. During the seventies, antiwar protests against American involvement in the Vietnam War swept college campuses. The students at Kent State were protesting against the United States dropping bombs in Cambodia. The National Guard was sent in to control campus unrest and prevent riots, and students were angered by their presence. When students began yelling and

tossing stones at guardsmen, the troops fired their guns. Four students were killed. Eight were wounded.

THE NASTIEST PLACE IN THE SOLAR SYSTEM

It's so dry, it makes the Sahara Desert look like a swamp. The clouds are pure sulfuric acid. What place is this? Earth's "twin," Venus.

On December 15, 1970, the Soviet spacecraft *Venera 7* landed on Venus. It was the first time a successful landing on Venus had been made. *Venera 7* sent information on the planet's surface conditions: temperature 455 degrees Centigrade (850 degrees Fahrenheit), pressure 90 bars (90 times Earth's!). No wonder the visit lasted only 35 minutes! Venus has now been visited by more space probes than any other planet. Yet it remains the most mysterious. Venus might be a nice place to visit, but it's no place to live.

NAME THAT TUNE

What were people listening to in 1970? The Beatles's two big hits were "Let It Be" and "My Sweet Lord." Simon and Garfunkel sang "Bridge Over Troubled Water." The Jackson 5 had a hit with "ABC."

STOWAWAY!

When 14-year-old Charles Semo-Tordjman's family moved from Paris to Australia, he took a dislike to his new country and decided to go back to France. He went to the airport in Sydney, Australia, and waited for his chance. He cried, "Wait for me!" as a family of strangers boarded the flight to Paris. Soon he was eating salmon in first class! Charles got to Paris all right. He stayed with an uncle until his father could save up the money to send him back to Sydney.

A woman bent over one of the casualties of the Kent State shootings

Gloria Steinem, one of the leaders of the women's movement, in her New York apartment

WOMEN CELEBRATE

The 50th anniversary of the passing of the 19th Amendment was a milestone for women. Why? The amendment had given them the right to vote. More than 10,000 women celebrated with a parade up New York's Fifth Avenue on August 26. They showed Americans that the women's movement was marching on. Bella Abzug, Gloria Steinem, Betty Friedan, Kate Millet, and other notable leaders made speeches. They asked for day-care centers for the children of working women. They asked for nonsexist advertising and equal pay for equal work. They urged passage of the Equal Rights Amendment, outlawing discrimination against women.

Twenty-eight-year-old Jimi Hendrix died of drug poisoning in London.

DRUGS KILL ROCK STARS

Two rock stars died in the autumn of 1970 from drug-related causes. Jimi Hendrix stretched the boundaries of rock with his revolutionary guitar playing. He played the guitar holding it upside down and behind his back. He strummed the strings with his teeth and with his tongue. No one since has been able to make quite the same sound. His career ended with his death from drug abuse at the age of 28. Janis Joplin, a passionate blues singer from Texas, died of a drug overdose on October 4 at the age of 27. Some say she was one of the greatest white female blues singers ever.

1970

GOLF GOOFS

On February 13, 1971, Vice President Spiro Agnew stole the spotlight from golf pros like Arnold Palmer. He was playing at the Bob Hope Classic when he hit two spectators, a husband and wife, with his first shot. On his very next swing, Agnew hit another person in the ankle. Disgusted, he jumped in his golf cart and drove off.

VOTE AT 18!

The voting age for Americans went from 21 to 18 on July 1, 1971, when the 26th Amendment to the Constitution was ratified. When he ran for president in 1972, Richard Nixon was the first president for whom 18-year-olds could vote.

ROCK STARS RAISE CASH FOR BANGLADESH

On August 1 former Beatle George Harrison gathered an all-star troupe of rock stars for a series of concerts to raise money for Bangladesh. Bangladesh was a new nation, born in 1971 out of years of war between India and Pakistan. Many of the people in this new country were homeless and starving.

More than 40,000 people attended the concerts in New York's Madison Square Garden. The concerts raised about $250,000 for the refugees of Bangladesh. Other performers were Eric Clapton, Billy Preston, Leon Russell, Ravi Shankar, and another ex-Beatle, Ringo Starr. The most popular guest was Bob Dylan. He made an unexpected appearance to sing on behalf of the refugees.

This was the first time a large group of rock singers and musicians formed a charity concert. Many more were to come in the seventies and eighties.

Joan Baez and Bob Dylan performed in Madison Square Garden at one of many benefit concerts given in the 1970s.

DRY LAND OR THE HIGH SEAS?

Drifting off to sleep on a bag filled with water was some people's idea of fun in 1971. Water beds soon became a nationwide fad. The mattresses had a few drawbacks, though. Filled with gallons of water, the beds were very heavy. Many fell through floors. Others split their seams and flooded the owners' homes. When temperatures dropped, the beds got cold and clammy. By 1972, most sleepers had decided to go back to dry land.

THE ROAD TRIP

Basketball players practice a lot. Some practice free-throws. Others do lay-ups by the hour. But dribbling in the two-foot-wide aisle of a bus is a whole other ball game!

That's exactly what Doug Melody, who played for the University of Connecticut, did in 1971. Doug was riding on a bus from Springfield, Massachusetts, to his school gym in Storrs, Connecticut, 65 miles away. The trip took one hour, 15 minutes, and three seconds, and Doug dribbled nonstop in the aisle the whole way. Off the bus, Doug continued to dribble to the basketball court. He stopped at the top of the key and shot the ball toward the hoop. Swish! It was a long way to go for two points. But he wasn't called once for traveling!

TERRIFIC TUNES

Janis Joplin's "Me and Bobby McGee." Three Dog Night's "Joy to the World." Rod Stewart's "Maggie May." Carole King's "It's Too Late." The Osmonds's "One Bad Apple." These were the top songs of 1971.

Janis Joplin singing the blues

Workers put the finishing touches on Cinderella's Castle at Walt Disney World in 1971.

THE MAGIC KINGDOM

Buckle your seat belt for Space Mountain. Explore Cinderella's Castle. Twirl at dizzying speeds in a teacup at the Mad Hatter's. Travel 20,000 leagues under the sea. Does this sound like a magic kingdom? It is! The Magic Kingdom at Walt Disney World, in Orlando, Florida, opened in 1971. In addition to rides and exhibits, it also offered lakes, resorts, hotels, campgrounds, parks, and stores.

13

1972

WATERGATE SCANDAL SHOCKS THE NATION

On June 17, 1972, an unusual burglary took place. It happened at the Democratic Party Headquarters in the Watergate building complex offices in Washington, D.C. Five men were arrested. It was later learned that the burglars were paid with money from President Nixon's reelection campaign.

The incident was investigated. The Watergate burglary turned out to be just the beginning. A network of burglars, informants, and troublemakers were acting on orders from high White House officials.

The nation was shocked. The scandal even reached the Oval Office. It seemed clear that President Nixon and some of his top-ranking officials were involved.

Left: Washington Post *reporters Carl Bernstein (left) and Bob Woodward helped uncover the Watergate scandal. Right: The Watergate complex in Washington, D.C.*

Former aide to the president H. R. Haldeman (left) and former White House attorney John Dean testified before the Senate Watergate Committee.

FINDERS KEEPERS?

What would you do if you found $500,000 in cash? Would you say, "Finders keepers, losers weepers"? Or would you think, "Honesty is the best policy"?

Lowell Elliot had to make a choice between those mottos in June 1972. He found $500,000 in cash on his farm in Peru, Indiana. It had been dropped by a parachuting hijacker. Mr. Elliot decided on "the best policy." He returned the money to its owner.

SPELUNKING, ANYONE?

Seven explorers in wet suits waded deep into Kentucky's Mammoth Cave on September 9, 1972. In the pitch dark, they made a huge discovery. They found a connection to a second cave. The two caverns combined formed the longest in the world.

A FINAL HIT

The youngest of seven children, Roberto Clemente always had worked hard and cared about others. He grew strong loading trucks and practicing baseball in his spare time.

In 1954, his hard work and talent on the baseball diamond were recognized. Clemente was drafted by the Pittsburgh Pirates. He batted over .357 and led the league in batting four times. In 1966, he was voted the National League's Most Valuable Player.

On September 30, 1972, Clemente slammed his 3,000th and final hit. Two months later an earthquake struck in Managua, Nicaragua, and left hundreds of people without food or shelter. Clemente, who cared about other people and his Latin heritage, organized an emergency airlift of food, clothes, and medical supplies from his home in Puerto Rico. Sadly, his plane crashed into the sea after takeoff and his body was never found. The world lost a great ball player and humanitarian in one blow.

OUTSTANDING OLYMPIANS

Olga Korbut won the world's heart at the 1972 Olympic Games in Munich, West Germany. After Korbut's flawless performances, gymnastics took off in a big way in the United States. Many girls wanted to perform like the young gold medalist from the Soviet Union.

Mark Spitz made a big splash for the Americans. He set world records in seven events. Spitz won more gold medals than any other competitor in Olympic history. He was swimming's new hero.

GET OUT YOUR QUARTERS— VIDEO GAMES ARE HERE!

In November, a company called Atari released "Pong," the first coin-operated video game. It was the beginning of a long-running craze. "Tank 8" came out in 1976. It was the first game with head-to-head action for eight players. In 1978, "Space Wars" became the first video game to use vector graphics. Next came a whole stream of "Pac-Man" games, talking videos, games using dual joystick controls, 3-D effects without 3-D glasses, and laser-disc games.

OUCH!

No one could believe it. Bob Hail, a student skydiver, dropped 3,300 feet at a rate of 80 miles per hour. And he walked away with nothing worse than a broken nose and a few broken teeth. After he had jumped from his plane, Hail quickly discovered trouble. Neither his regular parachute nor his back-up chute had opened.

Hail recalled, "I screamed. I knew I was dead and that my life was ended right then. There was nothing I could do." No one has been able to explain how he escaped unhurt.

Left: Olga Korbut's performance on the uneven bars at the 1972 Olympic games won her a gold medal and many fans. Right: Mark Spitz proudly accepted five gold medals.

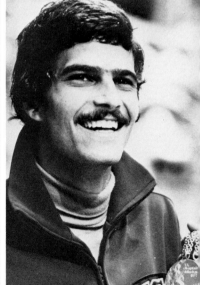

COMING HOME

The end of March brought troops and American prisoners of war home from war-torn Vietnam. America's longest and most costly war was over. The scars were many. The United States had lost more than 50,000 lives. Families and friends, as well as politicians, had fought over whether the country should have been in the war at all. It had been a ten-year struggle, and many people in America were relieved when it ended.

THE PEPSI GENERATION

In April 1973, Pepsi-Cola became the first American product licensed for sale in the Soviet Union. The deal started back in 1959. The late Soviet Premier Nikita Khrushchev joined then Vice President Richard Nixon for several ice-cold Pepsi-Colas. They were meeting at the American International Exposition in Moscow.

That moment of refreshment started better trade relations with the Soviet Union. Soviet kids like the same kinds of things American kids like. Since then, more and more American goods gradually have been allowed into the Soviet Union.

ADDRESS? SOMEWHERE IN SPACE . . .

What would it be like to live in space? How long could we survive? What would be the quality of our lives? These were the questions that prompted the United States to launch its first space station in May 1973. Named *Skylab,* it had two main compartments: a workshop and living quarters. Since there is no gravity in space, sleeping bags were attached to the walls.

Three teams of astronauts manned *Skylab.* They had a lavatory, shower, and solar-powered cooking appliances. They kept fit on exercise bicycles. When the last astronauts returned to Earth after a total time of 172 days in *Skylab,* the empty space station was left in orbit.

18

Finally, in July 1979, *Skylab* reentered Earth's atmosphere and broke up. The debris fell to earth. *Skylab* was an important step toward humanity's future in space.

KIDNAPPED!

The kidnapping of John Paul Getty III in June 1973 was one of the most publicized ever. Young Getty was the grandson of the richest man in the world. Four men seized the 16-year-old and drove off with him. But Getty's grandfather refused to pay the ransom. He thought the kidnapping was just a trick set up by his grandson to get money. Finally, in October, the brutal kidnappers sent one of the boy's ears and a photo of his head to Getty. They threatened to do worse unless the $2.9 million ransom was paid. It was, and still is, the largest ransom ever paid.

John Paul Getty III was released. The kidnappers were never found.

John Paul Getty III before his kidnapping

Billie Jean King helped Bobby Riggs jump across the net at a tennis match in New York. Riggs boasted that no woman could beat him. King showed him he was wrong.

BATTLE OF THE SEXES

When 55-year-old tennis pro Bobby Riggs bragged that no woman tennis pro could beat him, Billie Jean King couldn't resist the challenge. By the time she was 29, she had won the most Wimbledon Tennis Championships in history.

The showdown took place September 20 in the Houston Astrodome. The largest crowd ever in tennis history came to watch the match. Fifty million more viewers watched on TV. Bobby Riggs ate his words when Billie Jean King beat him. King won the $100,000 prize and a lot of respect!

OFF TO A FLYING START

Bonnie Tiburzi helped open a new career for women. In 1973 she was hired as a pilot for American Airlines. She became the first woman to fly for a major commercial airline. Flight attendant was no longer the only job in the air available to women.

PAY TAXES OR PAY CONSEQUENCES

On October 12, 1973, Spiro T. Agnew resigned as vice president of the United States. He was later fined and sentenced to

After the creation of better wheels, skateboarding made a comeback.

three years' probation for income tax evasion. Gerald Ford, Republican leader of the House of Representatives, became the new vice president.

ON A ROLL

Skateboarding started in the mid-1960s as a fad. Kids loved it. But it wasn't easy. Whenever metal or hardened clay wheels hit a bump or pebble, they stopped suddenly. The rider was thrown off. The fad faded.

Then in 1973, a California surfer named Frank Nasworthy had a brilliant idea. He put wheels of urethane, a soft plastic, on skateboards. The softer wheels had great traction and went fast. They didn't stop when the rider hit a stone. They absorbed shock and rolled easily over rough paths. When the boards were widened and dished out to make them more stable and easier to turn, skateboards caught on again. The fad was back.

1974

DON'T WAIT AROUND

Astronomers said Kohoutek would be the comet of the century. They told people to watch for its tail, 50 million miles long, blazing across the sky. On January 15, when the comet came close to the sun, it would be the brightest thing in the heavens. The head of the comet would glow five times brighter than the moon.

Kohoutek T-shirts were sold as people waited for the big event. But what did they see? Nothing more than a faint smudge in the sky. And even binoculars were needed to see that.

No one could explain the big gap between what astronomers expected and what really appeared. The comet was a dud—"the flop of the century." It won't return for another 75,000 years.

FREEZE!

Live mannequins, or "freeze" models, began drawing crowds to fashion stores in 1974. People had a great time trying to get the models to blink, laugh, or smile. But no one could "unfreeze" Mardeana Odom. On March 30, the 16-year-old Indianapolis model set a new record. Odom remained "frozen" for 5 hours, 32 minutes.

HAMMERIN' HANK

The number 715 was on everyone's mind the night of April 8 in Atlanta Stadium. As Hammerin' Hank Aaron stepped up to bat, baseball fans all over the world felt the suspense. The quiet 40-year-old had already hit 714 lifetime home runs. Could he break the record set by Babe Ruth and hit just one more?

The pitcher was Al Downing, hard-throwing and accurate. He delivered the first pitch. Aaron got a good piece of the ball and sent it sailing over the left field fence. Just like that, Hank Aaron had broken baseball's most famous record.

President Nixon announced his resignation on August 8, 1974.

Aaron was a great overall player. In his 23 seasons he had more home runs, more RBIs, and more sacrifice flies than anyone in baseball history. Because pitchers feared Aaron's great hitting, they also gave him the record in intentional walks. Hank Aaron's job as a young boy may have given him the best training for his baseball career. He lugged heavy chunks of ice. He developed the powerful wrists that could hammer a baseball over 755-foot fences!

NIXON RESIGNS

When President Nixon resigned from the presidency in August 1974, Gerald Ford became president. For the first time in American history, someone became president without winning a national election.

Ford's toughest job was to return trust to the presidency. In September President Ford used his presidential power to grant a pardon to Richard Nixon. Nixon was not tried on any charges of criminal acts in the Watergate scandal that led to his resignation.

Philippe Petit balances himself on a wire connected between the twin towers of New York's World Trade Center.

THE CIRCUS IS COMING TO TOWN . . . ?

The high wire act was unusual. There was no cotton candy, no popcorn munching, and no net. It did not take place "under the big top." Instead, it was done outdoors, between two sky-scrapers in New York City—the twin towers of the World Trade Center which had been recently constructed.

Philippe Petit, a 24-year-old from France, saw the towers as a high-wire adventure. On August 7, 1974, people craned their necks in amazement. They saw Petit cross on a high wire, 1,350 feet above them. Petit had shot the 140-foot wire from one tower to the next with a bow and arrow. He then performed for 75 minutes, crossing back and forth between the skyscrapers seven times. Police charged him with "criminal trespass," but Petit be-came famous. He was eventually convicted, however, and sen-tenced to provide free entertainment to city children.

I THINK I CAN, I THINK I CAN

Evel Knievel was a daredevil. His September 8 stunt had people shaking their heads in awe.

Knievel planned to rocket 1,600 feet across a canyon in Idaho on a motorcycle. Many thought it would bring certain death. It looked like they were right.

Knievel's motorcycle went streaking 1,000 feet above the Snake River. But a tail parachute opened too early. Instead of sailing over the canyon, the craft floated into it. His motorcycle landed nose down on a rocky river bank. The crowd below thought it might land on them! A rescue team pulled Knievel from the wreck. He had minor cuts and scrapes.

Before his memorable jump of the Snake River Canyon, Evel Knievel made a record-breaking jump in an indoor arena.

DO ROCKS MAKE GOOD PETS?

All you needed was five dollars, and a Pet Rock was yours. People in 1975 thought it was a great idea. Within months after they first went on sale, 250,000 Pet Rocks were sold. That was enough to populate a medium-sized city.

The idea behind this 1975 fad was to give someone his or her very own rock as a present. Rocks were different from your typical pet dog, cat, canary, or goldfish. Each one was neatly packaged in a box on which the name "Pet Rock" appeared. The fad lasted six months, but it was big while it lasted!

MONEY BACK

Automakers scratched their heads over their latest problem— poor sales. They were having one of the worst business slumps since World War II. They hit on the idea of rebates as a way to

A Pet Rock with its box and care manual

get folks to buy cars. Chrysler was the first to return $200 to $400 to anyone who bought a new car. Chrysler was followed by Ford and then General Motors, with rebate offers up to $500.

Too many unsold cars forced dealers to offer the bonus money. More than 200,000 auto workers had been laid off because of the sales slump. The gasoline shortage of 1974 convinced automakers that people would demand compact cars that used less gas. But the automakers made too many of the smaller new cars. The rebates, they hoped, would entice people to buy the compacts.

TREASURE TRAIN

Would you like to see George Washington's copy of the Declaration of Independence? Judy Garland's dress from *The Wizard of Oz*? These and more than 750 other artifacts were part of a traveling historical museum. It was called the Freedom Train, created for the Bicentennial, or 200th birthday of America. More than 30,000 people visited the Freedom Train in Stanton, Delaware, on its first stop. The train traveled coast to coast and visited 80 cities in 21 months.

WORLD WHALE DAY

April 28, 1975, was World Whale Day around the globe. Zoologists wanted people to realize that whales were endangered. There was growing concern over the killing of whales by Japan and the Soviet Union. Five species of whales were in danger of extinction. Several other species had been reduced to dangerously low numbers. "Save the whales" became a cause that many are still working hard to achieve.

"Bruce," a mechanical Great White shark, starred in the movie Jaws.

IN THE GRIP OF *JAWS*

It was a menace to swimmers. It was dangerous to those who hunted it. But it made a big splash at the movies. The Great White shark in the 1975 movie *Jaws* scared people in the theater . . . and sometimes off the beaches! The movie was so much terrifying fun that it became the second-biggest box-office hit of its time.

The movie shark was a 42-ton machine, coated with sand and equipped with teeth. Real sharks are not easily trained. They're also dangerous to work with. Filmmakers took their chances instead with a giant polyurethane model of "Jaws." It looked so much like the real thing that they fondly nicknamed it Bruce. Today, Bruce resides at Universal Studios in Los Angeles, where visitors still have fun being scared by him.

DON'T LEAVE HOME WITHOUT IT

Anyone wearing a T-shirt without words or slogans in the summer of 1975 might have felt naked. Plain T-shirts were out.

28 *After her historic climb of Mount Everest, Junko Tabei was greeted by an expedition of Japanese women who brought her supplies.*

Those with writing were in. The T-shirt boom advertised everything from beer to Beethoven, running shoes to the Fonz. And in many cities T-shirt shops opened that printed personal messages while you waited.

KEEPING SCORE

Americans love to keep score. Hamburger chains brag about the number of burgers they've sold. Baseball is famous for its scores and statistics. Announcers like to fill up the "dead" time between the pitches, hits, and innings with statistics about the players or teams.

On May 4, 1975, a new record was set when Bob Watson of the Houston Astros hit in the millionth run scored in baseball's major league history. Who knows, we may see signs under baseball's dome stadiums in the future reading, "Over two million runs scored . . ." Seiko Time Corporation predicts the two-millionth run will be scored in June of 2042.

TOP WOMAN

Junko Tabei, 35, made history on May 16, 1975. She was the first woman to conquer Mount Everest, the world's highest mountain. Everest had been climbed by 35 men since humans first scaled the Himalayan peak on May 29, 1953. Tabei, from Japan, brought the number of climbers to 36.

WANTED: STINKY SNEAKERS

Do you have sneakers with a good strong stench? Then you might want to go to Montpelier, Vermont, on the first day of spring. Every year since 1976, Vermont's state capital has been plugging its nose and welcoming spring with the National Rotten Sneaker Championship.

The stench of terrible tennies certainly hasn't kept people away! By 1989 Montpelier's contest had expanded to an international event. Winners of contests from around the United States, Australia, Great Britain, Canada, and Japan now compete to become the grand champion of stinking sneakers. Take a whiff of your sneaks. They might be a shoe-in at the next Rotten Sneaker Championship!

HAPPY BIRTHDAY, AMERICA!

What a birthday party it was! There were tall sailing ships, sizzling hamburgers, millions of guests, and booming fireworks. The United States celebrated its 200th birthday on July 4th. Everyone caught the spirit. Many Americans enjoyed the holiday by going to beaches, mountains, and parks for a peaceful time with their families. Millions of others went to public festivities.

These started on Mars Hill in Maine where dawn first reached the United States. As dawn broke in Baltimore, the "Star Spangled Banner" was sung at Fort McHenry. Fireworks exploded around the clock from coast to coast. In New York City, hundreds of thousands of people jammed river banks and roof tops. They wanted to see one of the most spectacular events of the day. Fifteen tall sailing ships and more than 200 smaller ones sailed from New York Harbor up the Hudson River.

In the town of George in the state of Washington, a cherry pie measuring 60 square feet was baked. Some Bostoners feasted on a pancake 76 inches across. On a hillside in Sheboygan, Wisconsin, 1,776 Frisbees whirled through the air. And in Washington, D.C., a million people cheered when lasers created the message, "1776–1976, Happy Birthday, U.S.A."

Tall ships sail into New York Harbor on July 4, 1976.

1976

A DAREDEVIL WITH A DREAM

How would you like a job where you are set on fire, drowned, or pushed off buildings? That's what stuntpeople do. Their jobs are to act in scenes that are too dangerous for TV and movie actors without special training.

One of the most famous stuntpeople is a woman named Kitty O'Neil. She has fallen 100 feet from a cliff. She has been drenched with gasoline and set on fire. On the 1976 TV program "Superstunt," O'Neil broke two women's records. She did the longest "fall" for a woman—112 feet—and did it while her clothes were on fire! O'Neil's stunt work has been seen on such TV shows as "Bionic Woman" and "Wonder Woman."

One of O'Neil's goals was to beat the women's land speed record. She did it in a rocket-powered car called the Motivator. It was a proud moment. But the stuntwoman did not hear the roar of the rocket or the cheers of the crowd. O'Neil is deaf. She lost

Left: Stuntwoman Kitty O'Neil. Right: Rumanian gymnast Nadia Comaneci

her hearing as a baby. She has always been determined to learn and excel. "I guess I like danger," says Kitty. "But, mostly, I want to always have a goal. I want to have some dream that I can try for."

IS ANYBODY OUT THERE?

Viking I was the name of the first pioneer to Mars. Instead of sending people, scientists sent a machine to study the planet up close. After an 11-month journey from Earth, *Viking I* landed July 20 on Mars. The *Viking* was the most complicated robot ever built. The probe dug into the soil and tested for signs of life. Its cameras photographed the Martian landscape.

Astronomers have probably spent more time studying Mars than any other planet. They think that besides Earth, Mars is the only planet on which life could exist. Some scientists believe Mars may now be like Earth was 200,000 years ago—an Ice Age planet. People have yet to travel to another planet. But robot travelers like *Viking* may help answer that old question, "Is anybody out there?"

PERFECT!

Just four feet, eleven inches tall, 86-pound Nadia Comaneci was the first person to receive a perfect score of 10 in Olympic gymnastics history. The gymnast from Rumania was 14 years old when she gave this rare performance at the 1976 Olympic Games in Montreal. She was competing in her first Olympics. Comaneci scored 10's on the balance bar, beam events, and the uneven bars. She took home three gold medals and a bronze medal.

Since then, a number of gymnasts have received perfect scores. That has made Olympics officials wonder whatever happened to the old saying, "There's no such thing as perfection." They're also thinking about changing the scoring system.

33

"THE KING" IS DEAD

Millions of fans mourned when the death of Elvis Presley was announced on August 16. Thousands flocked to Graceland, his mansion in Memphis, to weep at the gates. The rock and roll idol of the past 20 years had died at the age of 42.

In the fifties and sixties, Elvis had had stunning successes. Teenage girls screamed and fainted at the sight of him. Elvis had 28 gold records and more than 100 hits in the top 40. He had starred in 33 films. He had become the most popular American singer in the history of rock music. To millions, he will always be "The King" of rock and roll.

Elvis Presley in concert

NEVER STRIKES THE SAME PLACE TWICE?

An old saying tells us that lightning never strikes twice in the same place. But it can strike the same person twice—or seven times—as Shenandoah Park Ranger Roy Sullivan will tell you! The first bolt struck him in his big toe in 1942. He lost his eyebrows in a second strike in 1969. In 1970, Sullivan's left shoulder was burned. In 1972, his hair was set on fire.

In 1973, a bolt of lightning went through his hat, setting his hair on fire again! Are you counting? Sullivan's ankle was injured on the sixth strike. He was hit again on June 27, 1977, for the seventh time. Ranger Sullivan is a human lightning rod! He is the only person in the world to be struck by lightning seven times.

WILL THE REAL MR. JONES PLEASE STAND UP?

He narrowly escaped from four gigantic boulders set up as booby traps to crush him. He has stood perfectly still as deadly vipers slithered close to him, ready to bite. He is searching for the Lost Ark. His name is Jones . . . but not Indiana. His name is Vendyl Jones, and he is head of the Institute for Judaic-Christian Studies in Israel and Texas.

Jones and a friend, Phil Kaufman, worked together on a dig near Jerusalem in 1977. Later, Kaufman wrote a story based on Jones's experiences. His story was turned into the movie *Raiders of the Lost Ark,* which previewed in 1981.

The real Mr. Jones is now searching for the ashes of the Red Heifer. According to legend, once found, the cow's ashes can restore the magical power of the Lost Ark. Mr. Jones is following a treasure map based on one of the Dead Sea Scrolls. He hopes to find a bronze vessel carrying the cow's ashes. The Ark is said to be buried nearby. Good hunting, Mr. Jones. But watch out for sabers and poisoned dates!

THE SHOWBOTS ARE HERE

The 1977 movie *Star Wars* became the biggest movie hit of all time. As far as many of its fans were concerned, two robots stole the show. R2D2 and C-3PO won the audience's hearts. R2D2 is four feet tall, glides on the ground, and speaks in beeps, toots, and whistles. He is not humanoid in form. Shiny, golden C-3PO, on the other hand, is an android—a robot built to look and act like a human. C-3PO is over six feet tall. He walks, talks (1,000 galactic languages), thinks, and has feelings like a human.

THE SOUND OF CB

"Breaker, breaker, one-niner, this is Highway Host. You got a smokie at 297 on the double nickel." That's Citizen Band (CB) lingo. It translates as "Attention, listeners on channel 19. My code name is Highway Host. I'm warning you of a state trooper radar trap at mile marker 297 on Interstate 55." CB radios were so popular with truck drivers and hobbyists that they caused a national fuss. What was the problem?

Voices from highway airwaves were beginning to interfere with radio and TV frequencies. Congress and CB manufacturers were at odds over how to handle the problem.

Henry Winkler as the "Fonz"

THAT'S ENTERTAINMENT

In 1977, *Rocky,* starring Sylvester Stallone, punched his way to glory. John Travolta had *Saturday Night Fever.* Henry Winkler (the "Fonz") had "Happy Days." And the television miniseries "Roots" reached a record 80 million viewers. It was shown eight nights in a row.

HUMAN FLY IN THE SKY!

Thousands of New Yorkers couldn't believe their eyes. Were they really seeing a human climbing up the outside of the World Trade Center? Long before 27-year-old George Willig got to the 110th story, he looked tiny as a fly. Onlookers were thrilled, but the police were not. George Willig was arrested for his early-morning adventure. The City of New York sued him for $25,000. Willig used equipment he designed and built in secret at night. Why did he do it? "I just wanted the prize of getting to the top." The top was 1,350 feet above the streets of New York.

Left: R2D2 (left) and C-3PO. Right: Because CBs were so popular, this reporter started a special newspaper column about them.

Muhammad Ali jabs at challenger Leon Spinks during the first round of their 15-round fight on February 15, 1978.

SURPRISE FOR "THE GREATEST"

In 57 bouts as a professional heavyweight, Muhammad Ali had lost only twice. So when Ali stepped into the ring with Leon Spinks on February 15, 1978, he was a clear favorite. But this was not to be his night. Spinks was twelve years younger than Ali. He had won the Olympic light heavyweight title in Montreal in 1976.

To the amazement of Ali and his fans, Spinks was awarded the decision. Spinks raised his arms proudly in triumph, saying, "He may be the greatest, but I'm the latest." Exactly six months later the two faced each other in a match in New Orleans. This time Ali downed Spinks, winning his third heavyweight crown.

STEVE CAUTHEN RIDES HIGH

Steve Cauthen, at age 18, won thoroughbred racing's Triple Crown in June 1978. Riding a horse named Affirmed, he won the year's three biggest races: the Kentucky Derby, the Preakness, and the Belmont Stakes. It was a great feat for the young athlete.

HAPPY BIRTHDAY, LOUISE

Louise Brown of Oldham, England, was born on July 25, 1978. She was the first baby conceived outside the human body. The world's first "test-tube" baby, Louise was a happy addition to the family of John and Lesley Brown. Her birth gave hope to people around the globe who might never have had children without this medical miracle.

Steve Cauthen (number 3) crossing the finish line on Affirmed, winning the Triple Crown.

Benji, the lovable star of several movies

PAUPER TO PRINCE

It was just like the story of the prince and the pauper except the poor orphan who ended up with fame and fortune was a dog! His name was Higgins, a mongrel from a California animal shelter. Higgins was a scruffy but likeable blend of schnauzer, poodle, and cocker spaniel. When he cocked his head and fixed you with his brown-eyed stare, your heart melted.

Higgins's talents were discovered, and he was renamed Benji. Each of his movies made millions of dollars. In 1978, the dog from the animal shelter retired to luxury. Benji traveled first class on airplanes. He even dined at gourmet restaurants with his trainer. Benji could still do tricks for his admirers. He could open a mailbox and take out a letter, or yawn and sneeze on command. But Benji's best trick was still winning hearts!

WHO ARE THE ALIENS?

Where did human life come from? How did it arrive on Earth? Scientists have offered many theories about the beginning of life on Earth. But one put forth in 1978 is especially amazing. It holds that we, the people now on Earth, are really aliens! This theory was presented by Sri Lankan astronomer Chandra Wickramasinghe and English astronomer Sir Fred Hoyle. They suggested that we originated in space and were brought to Earth aboard a comet. How?

Wickramasinghe and Hoyle speculated that the creation of life was so complex that it needed the resources of space. According to the two astronomers, life arrived on Earth accidentally in the form of molecules. The "favorable conditions'" on Earth nurtured human life. Apparently, the molecules found Earth a nice place to visit and a nice place to live!

PLUTO'S NEW MYSTERIES

In 1978, astronomers at the United States Naval Observatory in Flagstaff, Arizona, detected Pluto's satellite, Charon. Pluto is the smallest planet. It is also the farthest from the sun, except when its orbit brings it closer to the sun than Neptune.

The discovery of Charon raised a lot of questions. Astronomers learned that Charon's diameter was about one-third that of Pluto—which is very large for a moon. They also learned that Pluto and Charon were the only planet-satellite pair that rotates and revolves together. So scientists began to question whether Charon was really a satellite. Could Pluto and Charon be a double planet instead? Or a double asteroid? Their mathematical calculations are keeping astronomers today wondering whether there might be another planet beyond Pluto.

PAPER DOLLARS, PLEASE

In January, the United States Mint began producing the Susan B. Anthony dollar. The new dollar was a coin about the size of a quarter. The government believed the new dollar coin would save taxpayers about $50 million a year. The coins would last longer than the paper dollars. The Mint could make fewer paper dollars. But the coin didn't catch on with Americans. It simply looked too much like a quarter. It wasn't easy for Americans to switch from paper dollars to dollar coins. The government took the hint and by March 1980 stopped making the Anthony dollar.

PATRICIA HEARST IS RELEASED FROM PRISON

In February 1979, President Jimmy Carter signed an order releasing Patricia Hearst, former member of the Symbionese Liberation Army (SLA), from a seven-year prison sentence. Patty, the daughter of millionaire publisher Randolph Hearst, was kidnapped by the SLA in 1974.

The SLA wanted to spread America's power and wealth among more people. They had said Patty would be freed if her father donated millions of dollars worth of food to the poor. Before she was released, Patty Hearst decided to join her kidnappers. She changed her name to Tania and dyed her hair red. She began to wear the SLA uniform.

In April 1974, she joined her captors in a bank holdup. In 1975 she was arrested in San Francisco. She was found guilty of armed robbery and served only 22 months of her sentence before she was released.

NUCLEAR MISTAKE

At 3:58 in the morning on March 28, hundreds of alarm bells shattered the night. The place was Three Mile Island nuclear

An aerial view of Three Mile Island, located in Harrisburg, Pennsylvania

power plant near Harrisburg, Pennsylvania. The worst nuclear power accident in United States history had just occurred. The accident was a result of both mechanical failure and human error.

It took workers several hours to discover that the core of the reactor was losing its vital cooling water. If the reactor had boiled dry and melted, tons of radioactivity would have been released into the air and ground. Thousands of people would have died from radiation poisoning. Thousands more would have died later from cancer caused by radiation. It was a narrow escape from disaster. It was also an extremely expensive accident. It cost nearly $4 billion to clean up. The accident taught us that reactors are only as safe as the humans operating them. The disabled and contaminated Three Mile Island could not be used again for several years.

SKATEBOARD SPEEDING

Good news for Richard K. Brown—there is no speed limit for skateboarding! He set the record for the highest speed (in a prone position) on June 17, 1979. He was clocked at a course at Mount Baldy, California, at 71.79 miles per hour. That's faster than most speeding cars.

HEAVY

Twins Billy and Benny McCreary were born in 1946. They were victims of a disorder that led to extraordinary weight gain. Billy and Benny were listed in the Guinness Book of World Records as the world's heaviest twins. They made the best of a bad situation by touring as a wrestling team. At one time or another, each had weighed as much as 770 pounds. Each was married, drove a custom-built Chevy, and took up two seats on airplanes. But in 1978, doctors had a warning for the 32-year-old twins: If they didn't lose weight, they wouldn't live another five years. Like many people, they had trouble believing their doctors. In fact, Billy gained another 40 pounds. He didn't live long enough to find out what harm that might do. In 1979, Billy was in a motorcycle accident and died from his injuries.

"That was the worst day of my life," recalls Benny. He quit wrestling and traveled with his wife. Benny then learned he had diabetes. He dieted and lost 526 pounds for the sake of his health. Benny felt like a new person!

SLAM, DUNK, CRASH!

Basketball star Darryl Dawkin of the Philadelphia 76ers loved to slam dunk. His height and tremendous strength made him good at it. But his slam dunk in the 1979 game against Kansas City turned into a shattering experience! The backboard broke into smithereens. The game was delayed 50 minutes while the mess was cleaned up and the backboard replaced. The National Basketball Association ruled against such slam dunks from that day on. Players who slam dunk now are out of the game.

Twins Billy and Benny McCreary

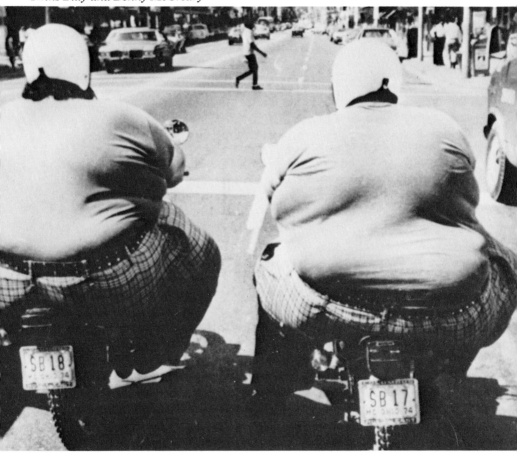

"Roots," the first television miniseries about a black family, starred Louis Gossett, Jr., (left) and Levar Burton.

INDEX